# I wish I'd TRAVELLED with MARCO POLO

*Written by Leonie Young & Avril Janks*
*Illustrated by Jon Gittoes*

*For my brother Harold - L.Y.*
*For my nephews Phil and Ben - J.G.*

WELDON
KiDS

# I Wish I'd Travelled with Marco Polo

Published in Australia by Weldon Kids Pty Ltd
565 Willoughby Road, Willoughby NSW 2068, Australia
A member of the Weldon International Group of Companies

First published 1995

Chief executive: Leonie Weldon
Project & promotions manager: Leah Walsh
Production manager: Cath Wadling
Designer: Astri Baker
Editor: Susan Scobie
Researchers: Avril Janks and Gabby Gleeson
U.S. researcher: Margi Kerns
Printed in Hong Kong by South China Printing Co. Ltd

© Weldon Kids Pty Ltd

National Library of Australia Cataloguing-in-Publication data
Young, Leonie
ISBN         1 875875 03 4 (hbk)
             1 875875 04 2 (pbk)
1. Polo, Marco, 1254-1323 - journeys - Juvenile fiction. I. Gittoes, Jon. II. Title

A823.3

Seven hundred years ago in Venice, a busy seaport in Italy, lived a boy named Marco Polo. Marco, who lived with his aunt and uncle, wanted to be a merchant like his father. He had to learn to speak many languages, how to buy and sell goods from other countries, and to understand different currencies.

Marco's father had been away many years in faraway countries to the east, buying silks, spices and other exotic goods.

Marco would spend long hours at the town's harbour talking to people and watching the ships arrive, hoping his father would be on one of them. Marco dreamed of the mysterious lands to the east that so few people had seen, and that held such riches of gold, spices, jewels and silk.

One day, as Marco sat at the wharf's edge, a stranger dressed in tattered clothes came and sat beside him. He smelt of the sea, and his luggage reeked of perfume and spices. It was his father.

Over the next few days Marco listened eagerly to his father's tales. He had been to Cathay, a huge land so far east it had taken years to travel there. Marco's father was the first European to meet the king of Cathay. The king's name was Kublai Khan. He ruled over millions of people and lived in a magnificent palace.

'I am going to return to Cathay,' said Marco's father, 'and this time you will be with me.' Marco's thoughts went wild as he tried to imagine all the things that might happen on the journey.

Marco and his father travelled by ship to Ormuz in Persia, by camel across burning deserts, and then over high, icy mountains. It was a hard journey. They had to eat strange, bitter foods and were chased by robbers. Marco became sick, but they continued travelling, determined to reach Cathay.

Finally, after they had been travelling for three-and-a-half years, a rider approached them. 'Welcome to the kingdom of the great Kublai Khan,' he said. 'The Khan has asked me to escort you to his palace.' They rode for 40 days through the fields and the towns of the Kingdom of Cathay.

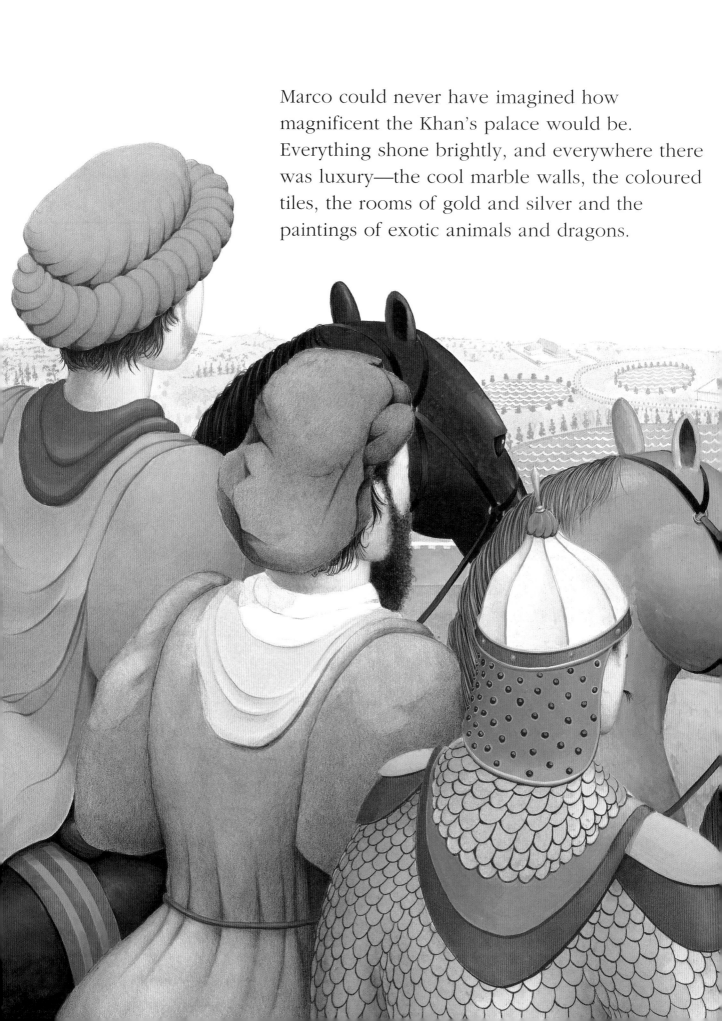

Marco could never have imagined how magnificent the Khan's palace would be. Everything shone brightly, and everywhere there was luxury—the cool marble walls, the coloured tiles, the rooms of gold and silver and the paintings of exotic animals and dragons.

Within the enormous walled gardens of the palace roamed wonderful animals. There were cheetahs, lynxes, tigers, deer, squirrels, and 10 000 pure white horses.

Marco felt very special as he walked through the palace to meet the great Kublai Khan. He was interested in all that he saw, and later wrote about everything in his diary.

The Khan was impressed with Marco, and soon they became great friends. Treating Marco as his own son, the Khan welcomed him into his royal world.

The palace was always filled with lavish feasts. The guests were entertained by performers of all types—from magic men and jugglers to acrobats and musicians. Marco loved it all, and made many new friends.

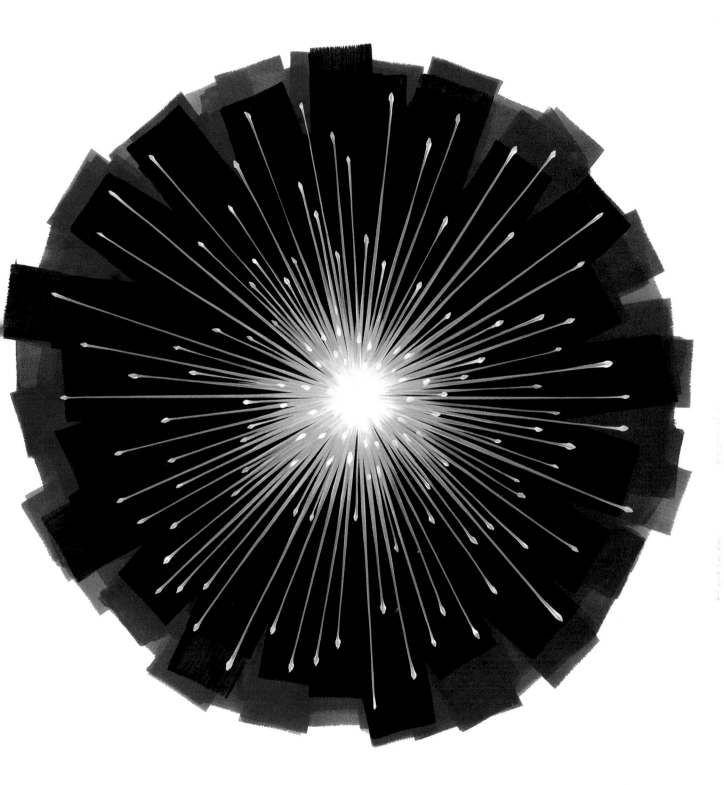

The Khan trusted Marco a great deal and made him his ambassador. This meant Marco had to travel across the kingdom, acting as the Khan's eyes and ears. He had to report back on what he had found and deliver messages in the Khan's name.

Marco marvelled at the wonders of Cathay, and the clever inventions of its people.

The people of Cathay were brilliant architects, designing enormous cities with wonderful bridges and buildings. One of Marco's favourite cities was Kinsai.

In all his dreams about strange places, Marco had never imagined anything as wonderful as this. It was a city of canals and thousands of bridges, which reminded him of Venice.
I have travelled further and seen more strange and fascinating places than any other person in the world, he thought. How I wish I could go back and tell everyone what I've seen.

Marco and his father spent many, many years in Cathay, but now Marco started to dream more and more of a faraway land to the west—home. But leaving the Khan was not so easy. 'I am very happy with your work as my ambassador, Marco,' he said. 'You report well on what you see and you can speak the languages of many people and travel great distances without tiring. Please don't ask to leave.'

No one would ever disagree with the all-powerful Khan—including Marco, and so he stayed. He had left Venice as an adventurous boy, and was now a man of many talents.

Finally, one day the Khan gave Marco and his father a very special job, one that would give them their freedom. They were to take a princess safely to another land, called Trebizond, where she was to be married. The journey was on their way home, and the great Khan sadly agreed they could continue back to Italy once the princess was safe. As Marco left, he thanked the Khan for all he had done for him—the wealth of knowledge, the royal life, the friendship and the trust.

After two long, hard years of travelling, Marco and his father finally arrived back in Venice. They had been away for 24 years, and no-one believed who they said they were or the great tales they told.

So Marco and his father held a big feast. On the table in front of them, they piled the spices, the silks and the gold ornaments they had brought home with them. They wore their old travelling clothes, and when everyone was sitting down they tore open the lining of their coats. Brilliant jewels from Cathay—rubies, diamonds, emeralds, sapphires—came tumbling out. Then people began to whisper, 'This man is Marco Polo, and he tells the truth.'

The great land of Cathay is now called China. As the years went past, the world learnt many things from this great nation.

These days we can all visit China by plane, travelling from anywhere in the world. But we can only imagine the riches of Kublai Khan.

If Marco Polo travelled the world today, he could take photographs, send postcards, and ring home whenever he wanted to.